MICHAEL L. SHERER

Good News for Children

Visual Messages on Epistle Texts Series **A**

AUGSBURG Publishing House • Minneapolis

GOOD NEWS FOR CHILDREN

Copyright © 1980 Augsburg Publishing House

Library of Congress Catalog Card No. 80-65553

International Standard Book No. 0-8066-1798-5

Scripture quotations unless otherwise noted are from the Revised Standard Version of the Bible, copyright 1946, 1952, and 1971 by the Division of Christian Education of the National Council of Churches.

MANUFACTURED IN THE UNITED STATES OF AMERICA

For Kathe
spouse and friendly critic
with love

Contents

Introduction

At a Christian writers' seminar in the American midwest not long ago, a workshop leader gave a one-page manuscript to participants around a table. "Tell me what seems right about this," said the leader. Answers came from everywhere: "The writer knows the Christian faith"; "The language is clear and understandable"; "Mechanics, punctuation, spelling all look right."

"Now tell me what is missing," said the leader.

The group fell silent. Finally someone said, "It tells the truth without imagination."

"That's right," the leader said. "How could we help this writer?"

More silence. The leader finally said, "He needs to do some windowing."

"Windowing?"

If you communicate the truth to others, you're a "windower." You look for ways to let new light stream in. You open "windows" in the minds of other people. Sometimes those windows take the forms of stories you have heard—they may be things that you've experienced. They may be stories you remember hearing somewhere.

Christians like to tell and hear the parables of Jesus. When Jesus told them long ago his listeners liked them too. His teaching was "well-windowed" with such picture stories. Modern storytellers know what Jesus knew: "a picture's worth a thousand words." A truth becomes dramatic, unforgettable when someone puts some windows in.

You're holding in your hands a "book of windows." Every story in the pages following is built upon Epistle texts (also called the Second Lesson) from the three-year lectionary. The story is a window you can use to cast new light on familiar truths. Every story uses something ordinary you can touch and hold and pass around. Many of these objects you may have at home, things you never thought could tell a story.

Some will use these messages at worship. Even though the sermon may be taken from the Gospel or the Old Testament, basing a children's message on the Epistle can add an extra ingredient to the message for the day.

Perhaps you'll use these messages in teaching. Children's messages like these work well in Sunday schools, vacation Bible schools, or anywhere a Bible-centered message seems appropriate in class or conversation. If you need some "windows" to communicate with younger people outside of worship (or at worship when your congregation doesn't use a lectionary series), borrow from this book in any sequence you desire.

Have a good time with this book. And, happy windowing!

Strange Armor

As you boys and girls have probably already discovered, it can be pretty rough sometimes living in the world. Sometimes you almost feel as though you should have some extra protection so you won't get hurt. In the Bible reading for today from Romans we are actually told to put on some armor. Who can tell me what armor is? What kinds of people do you know who wear armor, or who used to?

Well, today I have some armor I want to show you (*bring out the mirror and hold it over your heart*). What do you think? Would this give me good protection? It doesn't look much like it, does it! But now stop and think for a few minutes. Have you ever thought that a mirror could be a secret weapon? Well it could. I can use this mirror to hit any place in this room that you can see right now. Here, let me show you. Do you see that place way up there on the ceiling? Watch me hit it with my secret weapon (*take out the flashlight, turn it on, shine it into the mirror and watch the ceiling until the light is shining there*).

Objects: *a mirror (the larger the better, but any size will do) and a flashlight*

There, you see! Now, stop and think. If you were trying to protect someone how would shining a light with a mirror be able to help them? If they needed to see a signal it could help. Or if they were lost in the dark it could help. And if someone was trying to hurt you, I suppose you could even shine the light into his eyes and make him turn away *(but I wouldn't recommend that unless you really had to because you could hurt their eyes).*

Today we are starting the Advent season. God tells us to get ready for the coming light, Jesus, by putting on the "armor of light." He wants us to be ready to shine the light and love of Jesus all over our neighborhood—all over the world! He wants all of us to be just like a mirror. When Jesus comes into our hearts we can let him shine through us. Then God's gift to the world won't be wasted.

Let's use Advent to get ready for the light that's coming. And when it comes to us, let's let it shine!

Keep Looking

Have you heard the story of *Treasure Island,* written by Robert Louis Stevenson? It is a book filled with pirates and treasure maps and ocean trips and buried treasure. It's amazing how far some people are willing to go to try to find buried treasure.

Here's a treasure map. I don't know if it's any good or not. I found it in a secret pocket inside an old trunk up in the attic of my house. So it's probably worthless, don't you think? What's that? You think it might be the real thing?

Well, let's look at it. It shows California over here. And far, far over to the west in the Pacific Ocean is an island with an "x" on it. Do you know how many islands there are in the south Pacific? How would we know which one would be the right one? We could find a map of the Pacific Ocean and see if we can match this map with that one. But there aren't enough islands on this map to really help us. The only thing left to do would be to go to the south Pacific and start look-

Object: *A buried treasure map, with "x" marking the spot on a south sea island. Show the California coast about one thousand miles to the east.*

---

ing for the right island. And then if we ever found it we would have a whole island to search over. Who knows how long that would take?

Why would anybody go to all this trouble? Well, because they are sure that there is a treasure waiting. It might take them a long time and a lot of effort but they just keep looking.

We're a little bit like that too. During Advent we remember that God promises something valuable in our future. We are looking and looking for God's promises. One of them arrives at Christmas: Jesus will be with us. He promises treasures in our future. We don't know exactly where they are hidden, but we can live in hope because we have a kind of treasure map too. The Bible gives lots of clues about our world and what God is doing in it. If we listen to what we read and keep looking, believing hopefully that we will find it, God will show it to us.

An Ending
Worth Waiting For

Have any of you read this book? How many of you here don't know what the story's about? Well, the story is about somebody you would like a lot. Robin Hood goes through a lot of tough times but you get the feeling while reading the story that it would really be fun to be like that person.

One of the problems in reading a story like this one, though, is that there are so many times the hero gets into trouble that he doesn't deserve. He gets arrested by the sheriff who is really the one who should be arrested; he gets thrown into prison; at one point it looks like he will be killed. As you read those parts you can hardly sit still to listen to the trouble the hero is having.

Now there is one thing you could do if you are really impatient, or don't like to see how the hero is being treated so badly. What would that be? You could open the book to the last chapter and read how it comes out. Some people

Object: *A copy of* The Adventures of Robin Hood *or any other story that would interest young people, in which the hero suffers setbacks but succeeds in the end.*

---

don't want to do that because it takes away the surprise and ruins the story for them. But one thing it will do for you will be to help you to relax and put up with all the unlucky things that happen along the way.

You and I have a lot of unlucky things that happen to us every day too. Sometimes we get so discouraged we just want to quit. But we should remember something. God already showed us the ending. We know that God is going to send his Son into our life to take care of the troublemakers and give us a lot of good things we don't have yet but which we're patiently waiting for. He's coming. We know he will be here when we need him. Now that we know that our life has an ending worth waiting for, we can wade into the middle of the story, the part we're living right now, and not be discouraged.

Open Me First

Look at this unusual package. It has a gift tag on it that says "Open Me First!" Now why would a package say that? Do you suppose it's from somebody who thinks their gift is better than anybody else's so they want me to open theirs before the rest? That certainly wouldn't be a very good attitude for the giver to have, would it!

I think there could be a different reason for this tag. Who can guess? You think it could be a camera? That's a good guess. I remember seeing some commercials on television that showed "Open Me First" packages. They had cameras in them. The idea was that if you open the camera first, then you can capture the excitement of everybody opening other packages by taking pictures of it.

Let's see if we're right. *(Open the package.)* Right! Here's a camera. And we're in luck, it has film in it. Let's see if I can get a picture of this group of boys and girls—everybody get close together *(take a picture)*. Now I just realized that there

Object: *A gift-wrapped parcel in which there is a Polaroid camera with film inside. A tag on the package says "Open Me First!"*

---

are really two surprises here. The first one was finding out what's inside the box. The second one is finding out what the picture will look like. We'll just have to wait a minute to find out.

While we're waiting, let's think for a minute about the best gift of all. We are waiting all through Advent for the coming of Jesus. That surprise comes at Christmas. But in a way Jesus came in an "Open Me First" package. We already have Jesus. We met him at our baptism, and in Sunday school, and from what our parents taught us. But we know that he is coming back again, and then we will have a clearer picture of him than ever.

And speaking of pictures, here it is *(pass it around)*. We'll put it on the church bulletin board to show everybody how many came up for the children's message today. And it can remind all of you of two surprises as you wait for Christmas.

From God
with Love

Well, it's finally come! Today is Christmas. You and your family are really aware of what this day is all about. You have come to church to worship while a lot of people don't even bother about God on this day. They know it's a day for receiving gifts, but they forget that the gift is from God to us and it's Jesus.

Well, here's a gift I received. It had a note on it that said "From Dad, with love." Can you guess what's inside? Well, let me show you *(take out the weight)*. There it is. Actually he gave me an entire set of exercise equipment. He just wrapped up this small one to show me what sort of present he had hidden out in the garage.

What do you think? How is that for a present? Do you like to work out on exercise equipment? You do? You don't? Why? Why not? I have to admit, it really is a wonderful set of exercise equipment. There's just one problem. You see, I just don't like to exercise. I don't think I'll get much use out of this gift. At least, if I do use it I don't think I'll get much

Object: *A gift-wrapped box, containing a hand weight for exercising and building biceps.*

---

enjoyment out of it. I'm putting off telling my dad what I think of his gift because ... well ... the truth is, this gift is aggravating. Every time I look at it I feel guilty. In fact, I feel a little angry. You see, my dad gave me this gift because he knew I really need more exercise.

About the only thing that helps me is that little note that came in the box. It said, "From Dad, with love." And I know he gave it because he loves me. He knows that if I don't do something about my lack of exercise I'm going to be sorry some day.

Your Christmas present is like this too. The present we all received today is God's Son, Jesus. He came because God loves us. But by receiving Jesus we are agreeing to go on an exercise program for God. Jesus will train us to be in his family, not the devil's. If we accept this gift, it will do something wonderful for us. And it comes to us from God with love.

Ready When You Are

How many of you would like to have Christmas go on and on? Well, it does, you know. For at least twelve days after the 25th of December. And some people say that the season after that, Epiphany, is a little like a second Christmas season.

But I wonder if your parents feel like you do. Have you heard any of them say they would be glad when Christmas was over and gone? A lot of people say that. It seems as though many of us get so worn out doing so many things to get ready, and probably including a lot of unnecessary things we could just as well forget about, that we don't even appreciate Christmas and its meaning when it finally arrives.

I've heard people say, "I think Christmas just comes at the wrong time of the year." Well, I brought along a calendar today and I wonder if we could find a better time for Christmas to come. Do you want to help me hunt? Let's look at February. That would get Christmas a little farther away from where it is now. Would that be good? Some of you don't think so. February's too busy? Yes, there are some other

Object: *A Calendar*

---

special days in that month. What about April? Then it would run into Easter, wouldn't it? Summer time? You don't like Christmas in the summer? And of course a lot of you might be on vacation and would miss celebrating it with your friends.

Well we're not doing very well finding a better time, are we? Do you know something? There's no such thing as a "better time." That's probably why God didn't ask us when we wanted it. He just put it where he thought it was the best. I'm not talking about December now. I'm talking about Bethlehem and a manger. Some people didn't think Jesus was born at the right time either. Some wanted him sooner. Some wanted him later. Some didn't want him at all. But God just picked the best time—the Bible says the time had "fully come"—and sent Jesus to us. He knows more than we do about what makes the best time. We should learn to say to God, "You do things when you're ready. We'll be ready when you are."

Good Forever

Did any of you receive a gift certificate for Christmas? A lot of people like to give gift certificates because they want to give something useful but they don't know exactly what you want. The certificate is good at a particular store and can be spent for anything the store has, for as much as the certificate is good for. So, if I would give you a certificate for $5.00 to use at a drive-in restaurant you could buy hamburgers and malts there until $5.00 was used up and it wouldn't cost you anything. Or, if it was a $50.00 certificate at a clothing store you could use it to buy shirts and socks and suits or dresses and hats and purses until $50.00 had been spent and the certificate would pay for it.

I have a gift certificate here that everybody here can share. It was made out to all of you. Let me read it to you *(take it out of the envelope and read it)*. Now, that sounds great, doesn't it! Just think, this is good for whatever you need, both in this life and in the next one.

Object: *An envelope marked "Gift Certificate." Inside, enclose a certificate which reads: "This entitles you to whatever you need in both this life and the next, signed Jesus."*

Now, naturally, if you're going to spend this you'll have to find out what it is that "whatever you need" means, won't you. There's a catch here. Or maybe I should say a little "protection" is built in. God gives the certificate and God makes the promise but God also decides what it is that you and I need. It's a little like taking a certificate into the clothing store and having the clerk say, "Oh, the person who bought that for you told me what you should buy with it." We might not like that too well, but we should remember that God really knows what we need better than we do. And that's still a great gift, because God promises to take care of us forever. Even after we die and go to heaven. The Bible says that since we received Jesus as a gift from God we have every spiritual blessing. That's a gift that lasts forever. And God has already paid for it.

Everybody's Welcome

I've always wanted to be a king, haven't you? Well, I've got my crown on today and I'm ready to rule.

I guess it just isn't that easy. Being a king is something you have to be born into, isn't it. I'm really not wearing this crown to pretend to be a king, but to remind you that today is Epiphany, the day the three kings came to Bethlehem to see Jesus. You remember the story, don't you *(if some don't, refresh their memory).*

Actually Epiphany is about three kings who came to worship a baby king, Jesus. And then there was another king, Herod, who was at Jerusalem, and wanted Jesus dead. Herod knew the people of Israel were waiting for a greater king than he was and he was very nervous about new kings popping up out of nowhere.

But Herod wasn't worried about the three kings from the

Object: *A king's crown, made from colored paper or cardboard covered with foil. Wear it when you tell the story.*

---

east. That's because they weren't from Israel. And the Bible promised a king who would be born in Israel. So these visitors from the east could stop to visit Herod and not worry about him starting a war with them. They were foreigners. Herod probably thought they weren't as good as he was anyway.

That's one of the interesting things about these kings. They came to see Jesus, who was supposed to be a king for the Jews. But since they weren't Jews, why were they interested in Jesus? They must have figured out that Jesus was a special kind of king. They knew his kingdom was not only for Jews, but for everyone. In Jesus' palace *(it was only a stable or a small house)* everybody's welcome, no matter where they come from or what they look like.

That's good news for you and me too!

What's Your Name?

Is there anyone here today whose parents and grandparents and great-grandparents have always been Christians, as far back as you can go? Who thinks their family is like that? Let me see your hands.

Well, I have a big book here named "Original Christian Families." Now suppose I told you that if your family—your grandparents and *their* grandparents—have always been faithful members of Christ's church, their names would be somewhere in this book! Do you think your family's name would be in here? Let's look for some of your names in here and see.

(Begin asking each child "What's your name?" Pretend to look up their last names and solemnly announce that their name doesn't appear. Do this until everybody is eliminated. You might clinch it by announcing that your name isn't in there either!)

Well, I guess there just aren't any originals left any more. That's too bad. Because I received a phone call from the

Object: *A large book around which you have wrapped a paper dust jacket on which is lettered prominently the title "Original Christian Families"*

---

headquarters of our church last night and I was told that only the members of original families can sit in the pews from now on. All the newcomers have to sit on folding chairs in the back. And we can't give Holy Communion to any who don't have the right family names either. Only the originals can take it. So I guess everybody here is out of luck.

Do you believe all this?

Of course it's not true! But do you know that there was a time in the Christian church when some people thought that only "originals" could be Christians? That's right. And the church leaders had to decide if it was okay to let some newcomers join. The Bible says that Peter, one of Jesus' disciples, finally had a vision in which he learned that you don't use a book of "original families" to decide who gets in. Anybody who believes in Jesus can be a member. We baptize people from all kinds of families. We don't set limits. In the church of Jesus Christ everyone is welcome.

Be Sure
to Answer

(Hold up the Letter of Call) How many of you know what this is that I have in my hand today? Have you ever seen one? This is a Letter of Call. Who sends one of these, and who receives one?

A congregation sends a Letter of Call when they are looking for a new pastor. They will send this letter to someone who may be looking for a congregation to serve, or maybe even to somebody who isn't looking for a new congregation at all. Sometimes a pastor receives a Letter of Call from a congregation wanting him to come and be their leader and he is so surprised when it comes he has to take a week or two to get used to the idea and think it over very carefully.

Let's look at this letter. *(Open it up.)* You see, it has two parts. In this part the letter tells the pastor what he should promise to do for the congregation. All of it is really saying that he promises to be a good and faithful leader for them as they try to be servants of Jesus. Now here is the other part. The congregation promises some things also. They

Objects: *A pastor's Letter of Call and a Baptismal Certificate*

---

promise to help the pastor do his work, to pay him a salary, and to support him with prayer and encouragement.

When a Letter of Call is sent it is a way God can talk to somebody and invite that person to decide to do some special work for him. Teachers in the Sunday school often receive a Letter of Call also.

Do you know who else receives one? You do! I do! Everybody here today receives a Letter of Call from God. This is what it looks like *(hold up the baptismal certificate)*. You see, when you were baptized God called you to be a "saint" —that means somebody loved and washed by him. He also called you to his fellowship. That means he wants you in the Christian church family. You didn't hear or understand the call if you were baptized as a baby. But God keeps reminding you of the call to be a Christian every day. He doesn't forget about it. We shouldn't either. Let's be sure to answer the call by living his way.

Whose Side?

How many of you have brothers and sisters? How many of you are the best of friends with them all the time? I guess that's not so surprising. The idea of being in a family was God's idea, and it's a good idea, but sometimes it gets pretty tough to get along, doesn't it?

I've known instances where children in the same family have actually chosen sides to decide which of the brothers and sisters would be their friends, and which would be left out. You could walk down the hallway that led to the bedrooms in such a house and see signs on the doors like these two. (*Hold up signs.*)

And then, after a few days or a week, the sides might change, and somebody on one side would get mad and the sides would get rearranged, and maybe the signs would get changed, and things would go on that way for a while.

That sounds like a strange way for a family to behave, doesn't it?

What would happen if the house would catch fire some

Objects: *Two signs suitable for taping to a door. One reads "John's Side: Keep Out!" The other reads "Tim's Side: Keep Out!"*

---

afternoon while the two sides were having their separate meetings in their separate bedrooms, and one side discovered the fire but the other didn't. Now if the two sides were really serious about being opposite from each other I suppose the side that found out would try to get out of the house and not worry about the other side. That would really be a terrible way to be a family, wouldn't it!

Fortunately almost all kids grow out of taking sides with or against brothers or sisters. Unfortunately sometimes Christians don't. I once heard of some teenagers who wouldn't go to a youth meeting at church because other teenagers they didn't like would be attending. And adults can be just as bad. Sometimes whole congregations split up because people choose sides. The Bible tells us our business is to be on Jesus' side, and help him fight the devil. There's no room, or time, to choose sides among ourselves. We could destroy the family if we're not careful!

Where Is Wisdom?

Has anybody here ever been outside the country? How about overseas? Most of us have never gone very far across the world, although it's getting more common to hear about people taking world trips. Here's a map of the world. Suppose I told you that I wanted to find a city on this map where there would be sure to be wise people who could answer the complicated problems in my life. What city would you have me choose? *(Invite the children to pick out some locations.)*

I think a lot of people would pick out the capital of the country. Especially the capital of a big and powerful country, a country with a lot of money to spend on research and education. There should be a lot of wise people in a city like that.

If you would pick out the capitals of wealthy countries today where would they be? Washington, D.C., would be one. Here it is, next to the Atlantic Ocean. And you might choose Moscow, and maybe some of these European capitals, like London, Paris, and Rome.

Object: *A map of the world (or a globe)*

In fact, Rome was a capital city for one of the great empires of the ancient world, wasn't it? I'm sure in the first century many people went to Rome to find a wise teacher. But how strange it is that when God began to do his work in the days of Jesus he didn't begin by putting a disciple or apostle in Rome. Where did he put them? Well, one of them was in a place called Tarsus. Paul the apostle came from there. I can't even find Tarsus on here. And Jesus was born in Bethlehem and grew up in Nazareth. Those places aren't on here either! And the twelve apostles worked and lived in places that aren't on any maps today. God didn't hide his wisdom in the libraries of the big cities. He puts it into the hearts of simple people who know God's love and share it. Most of these people will never be famous.

That's true today too. We have people in Washington, D.C., and in our state capitol *(find it on the map)* trying to solve complicated problems for us, but often the real wisdom is found in little towns and villages where God's believers live.

33

Be an Instrument

Do you like to make things? Do you like to watch your dad or someone older use power tools in the workshop? Here is a power tool. What do we use this one for? Why don't we just use a hand tool to do the same thing without hooking it up to electricity?

There's something really fine about a power tool. It can do the work much faster and also much more faithfully, once we learn to use it properly. But wouldn't it be ridiculous if this power tool got it into its head that when it was working on a piece of furniture it would also be responsible for getting the design right? That's not the tool's job. That's the designer's job, the person using the tool. The only responsibility the tool has is to do the one thing it does best.

But wouldn't it be ridiculous if the tool thought that it was its responsibility to get itself plugged in, or to make sure the

Object: A *power tool. If possible, plug it in and be prepared to turn it on so that the children, at a safe distance, can see it operate.*

---

electricity was coming through? That's not the tool's responsibility. That's the responsibility of the one who uses the tool, isn't it? The tool's job is only to do the one thing it is designed to do, and do it faithfully.

You and I are like power tools, designed by God to do something special. What we can do is receive God's love and pass it on to people who need it. That's the love we were given when Jesus died on the cross. It is not our job to create the love *(just like the tool doesn't create the electricity).* We simply receive it thankfully and share it faithfully. It isn't our job to figure out fancy ways to prove that God's love is really valuable or that it really works, or to figure out fancy arguments to prove that God is real. Our job is simply to share the good things God has given us as faithfully as we can. We are instruments, tools for God. Let's be good ones!

Give It Away

Do you like to collect souvenirs? I do sometimes when I go traveling. Sometimes I bring home rocks or shells or pieces of wood to remind me of where I've been. Well, today I have two very unusual souvenirs to show you. Here, take a look, and tell me what they are.

These are souvenirs from two lakes. Why does the water look so different? You're right. One lake is pure but the other is filthy. In fact, you could say that one lake is alive and the other is dead. That's because in the pure lake fish and growing things can live. But in the polluted lake nothing lives any more.

How do lakes get to be living or dead? Well, in the case of these two lakes it was very simple. Both of these lakes received the same chance to live; both were fed from a river coming in, bringing pure water from the melting snow further north. But the two lakes did different things with the water each received. The one lake made a new river on the

Objects: *Two clear glass jars, filled with water, with lids sealing in the contents. One jar has clear water, the other full of sediment, impurities, and discoloration.*

---

lower end and let the water flow out again. The new river took the water the lake shared out to water the countryside and give life to plants the lake could not even see. As a result, pure water kept flowing right through the lake and because it was willing to share it always remained clean and living. But the other lake thought it was being wiser. It kept all the water it received for itself. It never shared any in a river that went out. What happened? The pure water it received became impure, and the selfish lake killed itself.

Sometimes people are like that. They fool themselves into thinking that the wise way to live is to do only things to take care of themselves and never worry about the life and needs of others. But that is not really wise at all. It leads to death.

Then there are those who receive good things but use God's wisdom. They share the goods they have. They have a pure, healthy life and others can live because of their generosity.

Keep It Clean

Is there anything special about this place where we are right now? We try to behave differently in this room from the way we do even in other parts of this same building. We don't do yelling or loud, foolish talking here. We don't like to have people running in this room. We don't like to have anything lying on the floor in here. And especially in the area around the table/altar we are very particular about how we move and act.

Why is this?

A worship area really is a special place, isn't it! It's a place where we meet God in a special way. We all know that God is present everywhere in the world, even in places where people don't even believe in God or listen to him. But there is something special about a worship area. It is a place where God has an appointment to meet us and talk to us and have a meal with us and welcome us into his family. There is no other place where things happen quite like they do here.

(If the story is presented in a place other than a worship area, the leader will want to adjust the message correspondingly.)

And so we give special attention to this place. We take care of it. We want it to be in such good shape that we would never be ashamed to welcome God here.

The Bible tells us that our bodies are like that too. We are told that our bodies are temples of God. He comes and lives right inside of us. Our bodies are special houses for him to live in. That's one way he can be close to us and keep in touch with us.

We should try to keep our own bodies as special and clean and ready for God to live in as we do this worship area. That means that we give attention to eating the right kinds of food, that we get enough exercise, that we don't put things inside our bodies that would make God's house impure. And we will always want to protect our bodies, and those of everyone around us, so that they are not treated recklessly.

Just think! We are a temple and God lives inside!

God Knows

It sure would be nice if we didn't need report cards, wouldn't it? But if we didn't have them you and your parents would have a harder time keeping track of your study progress. And it can be sort of fun to get a report card if you do well, or if the grades are better than they were the time before.

Here is a giant-sized report card. I made it up to show you how it might look if God prepared a report card for each of us. There are two subjects listed on this card *(hold up the poster)*. In the second lesson from the Bible today Paul tells us that God expects two things of his followers. One is that we are faithful servants. What do you suppose that would include? Probably doing our best to find out who is in need of help, and then finding the best ways to help them. If we're busy helping people who really need help we are getting very close to doing what God has in mind for our lives.

Objects: *On a large poster, draw a student report card. In-clude such information as Name, Subject, Grade. Under Subject, list: 1. Service; 2. Stewardship. Give each child a miniature copy of the poster, with the exception that on these smaller cards write "God knows" in the Grade column after Service and Stewardship.*

The second thing God expects is a little more difficult to understand. Paul says we are to be faithful "stewards of God's mysteries." What in the world might that include? I can think of two things. One would be that we should be careful how we learn and teach the special truths the Bible gives us. We need to handle God's promises carefully so we understand them correctly and follow their advice. The other thing could be that we take good care of Holy Communion so that we remember how special and mysterious it is, and remember to receive it faithfully and thankfully when we are entitled to come.

Now, how do you suppose God will grade you? Here's your own personal copy of the report card. You see, nobody can grade you except God. Only God knows how you're doing.

This Is
for Real

Almost everybody likes a story. Why do you suppose that is? Maybe because it lets us get involved in what the storyteller is talking about. When you hear somebody say "once upon a time" you can just about climb into that story and be a part of it, can't you? I've noticed that it's not just children who are like that. Adults like to hear stories too.

Well, I brought two books of stories along today. I am pretty sure that most of you have already heard or read most of the stories in both of these books. And yet, most of you would not be too tired of any of them to hear them told again, as long as the storyteller did a good job of telling them to you.

I want you to notice how different these two kinds of stories are. In this first book we have the kinds of stories that many people call legends or tales. They might have been created by people who were sitting in front of a fireplace or around a campfire or walking along a trail or going to market or just sitting under a tree.

Objects: *Two books of stories; one should be a collection of New Testament Bible stories, the other a group of children's tales such as Grimm's or Hans Christian Andersen's*

Here in this other book we have stories about Jesus. Nobody simply made up these stories. They are about a real person and things that really happened. They are a part of the history of our church.

Both kinds of stories have one thing in common. Both teach a lesson and show us a truth worth remembering. Even if a story never happened it can do that. Of course not every story teaches a truth—in fact, some stories are just for entertainment. But all of the tales in *this* story book *(hold up Bible stories)* teach truths and good lessons.

But we need to keep in mind the difference between make-believe stories and stories about Jesus, who actually lived and did what the stories say. When we hear stories about Jesus we should remember "this is for real!" We know they are because the first believers saw them happen, and they remembered, and saved the stories for us.

It Only
Takes One

Boys and girls, I have a very unusual looking street sign in my hand today. There's a story behind it. Let me share it with you.

Once upon a time there was a highway that ran between two lakes. Just at the point where the two lakes were quite close to the highway there was a road that crossed the main highway and led to both lakes. But part of this road had been washed out, and the part that remained sloped suddenly downward and then led off a sharp cliff into the water below. People unfamiliar with the road would drive along much too fast and suddenly find themselves racing downhill, out of control, and then flying off the cliff and into the deep water. At night it was even worse than in the daytime because the drivers couldn't see what was happening.

The builder of the highway became very concerned about this. So he built a bright signpost at the intersection and installed it just like this. He pointed the "Life" sign along the main highway and "Death" sign toward the lakes. He set it in a big hole, poured wet cement all around it, and then

44

Object: *A signpost such as would stand on a street corner with street names pointing in two directions. The pole can be a broomstick or mop handle; the sign boards can be heavy cardboard lettered in felt pen: one reads "Life," the other "Death."*

---

went away. Well, before the cement was dry along came a man who liked to fish and swim and boat and who knew that the side roads led to lakes. He decided that the road to the lakes should be called "Life," not "Death." So before the cement was hard he just turned the sign pole like this *(turn it)* and then let it harden.

Well, you can imagine what happened. People came along, looked at the sign, made a wrong turn, and ended up in the lake. It only took one person to lead everybody astray. Then along came the highway builder's son. He was alarmed that the sign faced the wrong way. So he dug it up and moved the boards back to the original direction *(move it again)*. Now people could live instead of die. Of course some kept going the wrong way. But at least they had a chance to go the right way.

God built the highway. The man who changed the sign is like Adam, the first human. The highway builder's son is Jesus. He came to lead us to life instead of to death.

The Best
One of All

Kids, if somebody came to your house and wanted to give you a score for being a good or a not-so-good family, how would your family come out? Would you rank higher than anybody else on the block? Would you be embarrassed?

One of the problems would be deciding how to measure who is good or not-so-good. Not everybody agrees on how to judge what it means to be a better family. Here's one way we could do it *(hold up the chart)*.

If we would use this chart as a checklist, would there be anybody here who succeeds in doing all four things for a whole day? What about a whole week? What about a whole month? Most families can't get all the members to do all four things even for one day.

Of course, you might say, "Well, what counts is who comes the closest. What matters is if you really try and succeed at two things, or even three."

Object: *A large poster entitled "How to Be a Better Fami-*
ly," under which these items are listed:
1. Do your jobs without complaining
2. Do something helpful once a day without be-
ing asked
3. Read the Bible or a religious book daily
4. Trust and love the leader

But would it surprise you if I told you that God doesn't require two or three things? He only asks for one. Which of these four do you think it is? If you said number four, you're right. Do I hear some of you saying, "That's too easy"? Not doing one, two, or three means you would get out of a lot of work, doesn't it? But notice something. If you do number four, you will soon be busy trying to do one, two and three. And you could do one, two and three but never do number four. Doing all the chores in the world isn't worth much if you don't do them out of love. That's why number four is the best one of all. That's also why in the Bible God said that Abraham and people who imitate him, by simply trusting and loving God, are more pleasing to God than people who do a lot of hard work but don't really love God at all.

Don't Step On Me!

Let's just pretend for a few minutes that we're all staying overnight at a Bible Camp somewhere and they've put us in a big room for the night with a carpeted floor and a fireplace but no beds. So we all stretch out and go to sleep in our sleeping bags. The fire finally dies and it's pitch black. Then I wake up and decide I have to find the bathroom. So I start across the room *(begin walking in the midst of the children)*. But pretty soon what do you think will happen? That's right! I could very well step on somebody *(you might playfully pretend to do this with a child whom you know to be a good sport)*.

Now if you were getting stepped on it would be very strange if you didn't say "Be careful! You're stepping on me!" But if I want to get out of the room in a hurry I'm going to have to find a way not to hurt everybody else. Now of course it will be inconvenient to everybody if I turn on the lights, but I could turn on a flashlight like this one *(turn it on; if*

Object: *A large flashlight or camping flashlight lantern, the stronger the beam the better.*

---

you have dimmed or extinguished the lights in the room, so much the better) then I can step my way through. I can be careful to shine the light at your feet, not in your face, and nobody should get hurt.

God tells us that living in this world is like walking through a dark room full of sleeping bags full of people. He wants us to try to learn what is pleasing to him. And Jesus taught us that what is most pleasing to God is that we help others and do not hurt them. Another way to say it would be, "Don't step on people." People who are God's enemies and don't care who they hurt will step on anybody in their way to get where they're going. They like living in the dark. God says to us that there's a much better way to live than that. We still might make some mistakes even if we use the light of God's love in Jesus. But yet this is the best way—it is the only way!

What's On Your Mind?

If you could have any wish you wanted, what would you wish for? What would you most like to have, or to have happen in this world? The way we answer that question will say something about what's on our mind, what sorts of things we think about.

I brought along a "Wish Book" today. Inside are some examples of what a lot of people would like to use their wish for if they had one. Let's look at some of the things inside. *(Turn the pages, let the group comment on what they see, why someone would wish for that, who would be helped or hurt if the wish was granted, and how it would change the life of the person wishing for it. Go no further than the last item in the first section, picturing expensive luxuries.)*

Now, what is on my mind if I wish for one of those kinds of things? I would be pretty interested in looking out for my own comforts, wouldn't I? What happens when we do that?

Object: *A scrapbook you have prepared. It can be made simply with several pages of 8½ x 11 paper fastened at one side with string or ribbon. The cover or first inside page should be entitled "Wish Book." The following pages picture expensive material goods and services, including some luxuries. The last pages picture situations in which the poor are being helped.*

Do you suppose we would have any trouble remembering what our purpose is in this world if we did that? Would we become so selfish and separated from less fortunate people that we would be impossible to live with? Would we forget about God or decide we didn't need him any more?

The Bible says we would. St. Paul says these are "things of the flesh." That means, things of this world that don't last and don't really matter very much and get in the way of living the way God wants us to. He says we should try to set our minds on something quite different. He calls them "things of the Spirit." Let's look at some more pages in the "Wish Book." *(Look at the other pages.)* When the Spirit of God is in us then we have our minds set on doing what God wants to get done, like helping our neighbors live better and helping the poor. That's worth wishing for!

Follow the String

When I was growing up some parents would surprise their kids on their birthdays by hiding a special birthday present somewhere in the house and then tying a string to it. The string would be trailed around and around through hallways and sometimes even out of the house and back again. If the present was too big to wrap up this was an especially good way to present it to the child. At just the right moment the parent would give the end of the string, just like this one, to the child and say "Now just find the end of the string and you'll have a surprise." And off the young person would go, rolling the string up as the search continued.

Just suppose mom or dad gave their child the end of a string and the child said "Aw, that's silly. I'm not going to play this crazy game. Besides, it's probably a trick." For all that child knows, it could be a new bicycle. But the child will never find out except by following the string.

God asks us to follow even though we don't know where

Object: *A long string which is tied to something in a room through a door and concealed from the group where you are standing (if you have no doors where you are standing, have an usher bring the string down the aisle, attached to something through a door elsewhere in the building). On the end of the string you are holding is a cardboard sign that says "Follow me."*

---

we will end up. He gives us his Spirit and his Spirit pushes and pulls and urges us to follow him. He leads the way and begs us to come after him. It's like following a string. You never know where it will go. It may turn corners and climb stairs and go out of the house, or behind the couch and out again. You don't dare stop and say "I'm getting tired of following." You won't have the good part until you get to the end.

Why should we follow when we don't know where we will end up? The best reason is because we were asked to by somebody we know and trust. The birthday string was given to us by our parents. We know they do things because they love us. God asks us to follow where his Spirit leads because our lives will be richer and better and safer. We can trust God, so we can follow his Spirit even if we don't know where we will end up. God is like our parents. We are in his family. We can follow him anywhere.

I'll Do
the Dirty Work

Have you ever gone exploring in a cave? It's not a good idea to go by yourself and it's not a good idea to go without telling someone else where you are going. I want you to suppose that two of your friends have gone exploring in a cave. You didn't go along but you know where the cave is. They promise to be back by three o'clock at the latest. It's four o'clock and they have not come back. You and another friend are worried now so you hike out to the entrance to the cave and look in and call their names. They echo loudly and disappear down into the darkness. But nobody answers.

Now you have to decide how to find them. You agree with your friend that one of you will have to go in and look and try to find them. That person will need to carry a flashlight lantern like this one and unwind a roll of twine like this so at least the searcher doesn't get lost too and can't get back out. The other one will stay out on the outside and make sure the end of the twine doesn't get pulled inside the cave.

Objects: *A large flashlight lantern, the type that uses one large square battery, and creates a broad beam. Also, a ball of twine.*

Now the problem is to decide who will stay outside, where it is safe and clean, and where one can control the rescue operation, and who will go inside where it's dark and dirty and dangerous and do the rescuing. Now suppose the two of you simply argue with each other about who will stay outside and control the operation. Nobody would ever go in and nobody would ever be rescued. Let's say that you finally agree, "I'll do the dirty work. I'll go in there and rescue them. You just be sure to keep the end of the twine safely secured here at the entrance and come in along the line to rescue me if necessary." Then you can get down to business saving the others.

Jesus and his Father in heaven are both helping to rescue us from sin and the devil. But one of them needs to be in control in heaven. That's God the Father's job. But Jesus says "I'll do the dirty work." And he did!

It Lasts Forever

Let's have some fun! I have a poster here today with all kinds of choices on it. I'd like to have you pick just one of these as the one that would give you the most happiness, both now and in the next ten years. What most interests you? *(Let them choose, encourage them to tell you why they pick what they do.)* Any one of them looks like a lot of fun, don't they? Oh, wait a minute, what about this one here? It doesn't seem to fit in with the others. I suppose if you chose that one it wouldn't be much of a prize. Did anybody pick it?

Now that everybody has something picked, let me ask you another question about the choice you made. Do you think it would be satisfying to you after ten years? Fifteen? Thirty? Would you get tired of it? Would it possibly turn your attention away from other more important things and make you forget to care about some things you should?

There are really two kinds of choices on this poster: all but one of them can be described as "things that are on

Object: *A large collage poster, picturing 8 to 10 items that appeal to a consumer society: large car, fancy house, motorboat, swimming pool, etc. In the collection somewhere picture a starving child or someone who is obviously hurting.*

---

earth." They really aren't very important. They really don't last. You can have a nice house or car or swimming pool or boat but you can get tired of them. They can even get you into trouble because you spend too much money on them and forget about important things.

But there is one other thing here. See it? It's the person who is hurting. That person needs love. When we pick that kind of choice to spend our time and our energy as being more important than anything else, we have chosen something that is "from above." It is the kind of thing that God is all about, and that Jesus wants us to think about and do something about. It's easy to fall in love with comfortable, expensive things on earth. But now that Jesus is raised from the dead he has given us a special new kind of life too. And in our special new life we don't have to get trapped just loving a lot of things that don't really matter, and that might get us in trouble. We can do what Jesus does: love other people. That will last forever!

Ready and Waiting

How many of you pack a lunch to take with you every day? Lots of people do, including a lot of moms and dads who take their lunches along to work with them. We all know how we look forward to lunch time so we can go and get our lunch and open it up and enjoy what's inside. If somebody fixes your lunch for you, it is probably a sort of surprise to find out what is packed inside from day to day. If you take a lunch in a lunch box there's almost always a sandwich inside.

Suppose you opened your lunch box one noon to eat, and you were really hungry, and had been looking forward to eating for about an hour, and what you found was this! *(Take out the stale sandwich.)* Now that's the kind of surprise we can all do without! What's wrong with this sandwich? *(Let them handle it if they wish.)* It surely wouldn't taste very good, would it? Somebody forgot to put the protection around it. It wasn't wrapped in a sandwich bag. Now it's so

58

Objects: *A school lunch box, inside which are two peanut butter sandwiches, one wrapped in lunch wrap and kept fresh, the other not wrapped and with hard, stale bread.*

---

hard and stale nobody would want it. But it was perfectly good when it was made the night before.

Now this would be more like it. *(Take out the sandwich kept fresh.)* Whoever prepared this sandwich remembered to keep it fresh and ready for eating. If somebody promised to make you a lunch and then wrapped it up like this it would be a promise well kept.

God makes a promise like that. He says that we should be faithful to him while we live in this world because he has something special in store for us. Wouldn't it be a disappointment if what God promised wasn't worth much or that it had gotten old and useless while we were waiting to receive it! But God doesn't do that. The Bible says he has an inheritance for us which is imperishable, undefiled, and unfading, kept in heaven for us. We need to be patient until we can receive it. But we need to trust God to keep his promise too.

What a Prize!

Let's pretend that you have done something to hurt me. Now I am angry at you. We haven't been speaking much to each other. I avoid you whenever I can. All of this has upset you terribly and you are trying to find a way to put things back together again and make them right like they were before.

Finally one day you come to me and say, "Listen, I just can't go on like this any more. What can I do to satisfy you that I am truly sorry? I'm even willing to buy back your friendship if I have to."

And so I think about it. And I know that friendship is never really "for sale," but I decide that if I let you pay for it somehow it would at least show how serious and sincere you are about it, and it would be a good lesson to help you avoid doing it again. So I answer "Well, if you can come up with

Object: *A stamp collection, preferably a set of first-day covers (stamps on specially cancelled envelopes); a set of select rare stamps which are otherwise special and distinctive will work well also.*

---

just the right peace offering, I'll forget about it and we'll call it even."

And then you begin to think of something that would be good enough to give. And finally you come up with this *(hold up the stamp collection)*. And you say to me, "Now you might not like stamps, but I want to tell you some things about this collection. And even if you don't like stamps, you'll realize that it would be valuable if you wanted to sell it, because of all the special things about it." *(Mention some of the things that make the collection really special.)*

And when I hear from you what makes the collection so perfect, all I can do is say to you "Wow! What a prize! This really proves that you are serious about being friends again!"

That's the way God works for our friendship. Things are turned around with God and us, though. We did the wrong, but God comes up with the perfect gift. He gives us Jesus.

Look for
the Footprints

Is there anybody here today who could wear this pair of shoes? They're really too big for any young people, aren't they! They're even too big for a lot of adults! The person who wears this pair of shoes could probably do a lot of good, hard work.

Now, just imagine you were supposed to follow somebody across difficult hilly country on a snowy winter day. Which kind of footprints would you prefer to follow, big ones like these or prints from small shoes? Of course, if they were small like your shoes it would be easier to keep pace—you wouldn't have to stretch so far in between. But maybe these big footprints would really be better, because they would be heavier and deeper and easier to see. You wouldn't get lost so easily. You might have to take two steps to match every one step made by the person wearing these, but you could be sure you were on the right trail.

Object: *A pair of very big workshoes.*

Jesus wears shoes like these. He left footprints so big and so deep that we can't miss them. We can't keep up with them either. He did his work so well and so completely that we can never do as good a job as he did. When he said "love your neighbor" or "suffer for your enemies" he went all the way to the cross—he died to do it. None of us, including us adults and parents, can do that. But we can look for his footsteps and follow along where they lead. The Bible says to us "Christ suffered for you, leaving you an example, that you should follow in his steps." I'm glad that Jesus' shoes are so big. It doesn't bother me that I can't make footprints as deep as he did. If I can make footprints that go in the same direction that's good enough. It doesn't bother me that I can't travel as far or as fast as Jesus did. I can still go the same places he did. That's good enough. God just wants us to look for the footprints, and follow!

Can I
Count On You?

Have you ever played with building blocks? Maybe you did in school or maybe you have some in your playroom at home. It's really fun to build things with building blocks. Here's a picture this morning of how you can use blocks to build a wall. You notice that these blocks in the second row depend on the ones on the bottom row. And every block rests on two other blocks. That's so the wall is stronger. It spreads out the weight of these higher up and makes each one depend on not just one but on two below it.

Now just suppose somebody came along and took one of these stones out of this row and left a hole right here. What would happen to the wall? Would it fall down? Not necessarily. Since the other stones are all overlapping each other the wall might still stay together. But it would be a lot weaker wouldn't it!

Object: *A large piece of poster board on which you have drawn with simple lines the interlocking pattern of a stone wall. Show at least four layers of stone, with each stone overlapping two others. If you can, show a corner and the beginning of a second side of wall going off at a right angle.*

You and I are like stones in a wall. The Bible says we are to be like living stones. When we support each other as Christians, helping each other to do what is right, looking out for each other when one of us gets into trouble, we are like a strong wall like this. Except that every stone is really alive. When one of us gets mad and decides to pout and not help anybody else, we become like a stone that decides to leave the wall. God needs all of us to build up his church. It's bad enough if we tell him he can't count on us any more, but what's worse is that the other people in the wall who have learned to count on us can't depend on us either. And that may mean real trouble. Once we all get built into the wall, we really need each other.

This cornerstone is Jesus. We can always count on him. Can he count on us?

What Do You Mean?

I have a message for you this morning that is really tremendous. Is there someone here who can read who would like to tell us what it says? *(Try to locate someone who at least knows the alphabet. Let them study the page for a moment.)* Actually, what it says there is something that you've heard before. Can you tell us what it is?

There's a problem here, isn't there. This is a copy of the Bible, but it isn't written in our language. It's written in Greek *(or whatever language you have).* How are we going to get the message if we don't understand the language? That's right, somebody will have to translate it into English. Did you know that when the Bible was first written down it was not in English? It was in Hebrew and Greek. Later on it was in Latin. In the 1600s Martin Luther translated it into German. We're lucky that we have the Bible in English.

Now I'm going to give you a clue. The part I asked you to read is John 3:16. Can anybody say it? *(If they can't, you recite it.)* Does that sound familiar to you? Most of us have

Object: *A copy of a Greek New Testament or any foreign-language Bible or New Testament. As the children gather, open the book to John 3:16; you might consider drawing a box around the verse.*

---

heard those words often. If a friend who doesn't know Jesus wanted to know why you believe in him, you could tell him what it says in John 3:16. It wouldn't help if you gave him a Greek Bible and said, "Here, read this. It will explain everything." God tells us that we should be ready at all times to account for the hope that is in us. That means be ready at all times to explain why we trust God. Sometimes we hear people say "I know what I believe but I don't know why." Or they will say "I just take everything by faith. I can't explain any of it." If they said that to me it wouldn't convince me to believe what they do. I need to know more. I want to know why people believe it.

You and I need to be ready, if anybody asks us, to tell them why we believe in Jesus. It wouldn't help to say "I don't know; I just do!" We can say "Because he loves me" or "Because he died for me." Maybe you have an even better answer.

A Scar to
Be Proud Of

Boys and girls, how many of you have a scar somewhere? We get scars in lots of ways, don't we. You could get one from an accident, or from having an operation at the hospital, or even from being in a fight.

Take a look at this scar for a minute. Where do you think it came from? *(If it is your scar, or the scar on a person about whose history you know, tell about it. If it is a scar on a person in a picture, do some creative imagining with the group.)*

Do you think having a scar is something to be proud of? Is it something to be ashamed of? It might surprise you, but either answer could be correct. It all depends on why you have the scar. If you got your scar from having an operation in the hospital, you could probably be proud of that scar because it shows that you trusted the doctor to help you get well, and it might prove that you were brave. In fact, a lot

Object: *A scar on the body of the storyteller, visible to the group; or, a scar on a child you are sure will be present; or a scar on another person who consents to be present at story time; or, a picture of a person with a prominent scar visible.*

---

of boys and girls like to show off their hospital scars to their friends.

But maybe you got your scar from having a fight with somebody when there should never have been a fight in the first place. All of us know somebody who acts like a bully and is actually proud of getting into fights with people. If these people get scars from fighting, they probably think they are a badge of honor. People who know Jesus know better than that: those scars are nothing to brag about because they resulted from hurting, not helping people.

In the Bible we are told that there are two kinds of trouble you can get into, and two kinds of scars you can get. If we are hurting people or disobeying God we shouldn't brag about the trouble we have. But if we have trouble and scars from loving and helping others, that's trouble to be proud of. Make sure your scars are the right kind!

69

Housecleaning Time

Kids, what's the strongest wind in the world? *(Field some answers. You'll get: blizzard, hurricane, typhoon, tornado.)* How do you feel about really strong winds? They can be scary, can't they? Most people who hear that a tornado is coming will head straight for the basement. A tornado is so strong that not only will it carry away things that are loose and cluttering up the countryside but it will also tear loose things that are fastened down. It's like an enormous vacuum cleaner.

I have a vacuum cleaner here this morning. Some of you have this kind at your house. A vacuum cleaner is something like a tornado too, isn't it? It creates a wind inside and the wind scoops up everything in the way of this nozzle when you point it at a place where there's dirt to be picked up. How do you feel about vacuum cleaners? Is it different than your feeling about tornados? Why is that? *(Talk about it.)*

There are at least two things I can think of that make me feel good about vacuum cleaners. The first one is that they

Object: *A vacuum cleaner, cannister type with wand and nozzle attachment. If not convenient to bring the cleaner, just bring the attachment.*

---

almost always pick up things we want to get rid of. They do good things, not bad things *(like tornados usually do)*. The second thing is that a vacuum cleaner is a wind that's under control. You can use it exactly how and when and where you want to.

That's the way God works. He moves through the world like an enormous vacuum cleaner getting rid of the dirt in our lives. This is what God's Holy Spirit does. He moves about like a good tornado, getting rid of the things that keep us away from God and make us forget to live for God. God introduced this wonderful big wind at Pentecost just after Jesus had gone back into heaven. The disciples were waiting for something to happen to convince them that God was still with them. All of a sudden there was an enormous rushing wind, just like ten thousand vacuum cleaners. It was the Holy Spirit. The Spirit cleared the way for the disciples so they could do good work for God. That's what God's Spirit does for us too.

71

God's Family

Boys and girls, I have something special in my hand today. How many would like to have part of it? *(Peel off the label backing and fasten one label to the forehead of each child who raised a hand. If some did not, do not put a label on. Be certain that the leader fastens the labels, not the children.)* Now, do any of you know what I just put on your forehead? If you're not sure, ask your neighbor to tell you what it is *(give them a few seconds)*.

Now I want to read you something *(Open the "I Promise" and read)*: "I promise that any person who has my special sign on his or her forehead, and who keeps on wearing it, is entitled to be a part of my family. They may come to a great banquet I am planning and share everything that is mine. Signed, The Great King."

How many of you would like to receive what I just read? How many of you would be willing to leave your mark on your forehead in order to receive it? What do you suppose

Objects: *Some small self-adhesive labels (the peel-off type) on each of which is drawn a cross; prepare enough for the number of children expected. Also a sheet of paper folded in thirds, marked on an outside panel "I Promise." The inside text is given below.*

---

would happen tomorrow if somebody saw you walking down the street wearing it? It might surprise some of you, but all of this has already happened. How many of you have been baptized? If you are baptized, you already have the same mark on your forehead. Jesus put his cross on you. He made you a part of the family of God. God is saving good things for you when you join him in heaven. How did we get into this family? The same way you just got the mark on your forehead. Somebody gave it to you. That's what the Holy Spirit does in Baptism. How did you find out what the mark was? Somebody else told you. That's what the Spirit does too. The Holy Spirit helps us to know who our heavenly Father really is. He encourages us always to wear our mark like a badge to be proud of. It's a way of saying God is our Father.

The Apostle Paul wants us to think of ourselves as brothers and sisters in one big family of God, to love one another, and to live in peace. This is God's will for us too.

They're Both
Worth the Same

Boys and girls, I have two pieces of art in my hands. Which one is best? *(Let them vote.)* Why did you choose that one? Does one of them look as though it were painted by a more skillful artist than the other?

Suppose I told you that both of these artists are exactly the same age and that both are in the same school class and have learned the same things about art from the same teacher. Would it change your opinion about which picture is best? Do you think one artist should brag about his or her art work and the other one should be ashamed?

That would be a perfectly natural reaction. And that is exactly the way we evaluate most things in our life. The person who can hit home runs gets our praise. The one who strikes out gets ridiculed. When a Boy Scout gets the Eagle

Objects: *Two paintings of unequal comparison, one of which should be immediately more appealing to the children. If possible, two paintings done in watercolor by students in the same age or class group, but of contrasting quality, would be best. Or the leader can prepare two paintings for this message.*

---

award we think he is entitled to brag. If he can't get past Second Class we think he should be ashamed of himself.

Guess what! God says that's all wrong! The only people who are allowed to brag are the people who do their skill perfectly without any mistakes at all. Do you know anybody like that? I don't. You might say, "But what if we do the best we possibly can? Doesn't that count?" Take another look at these two pictures. Both of these artists did the best job they possibly could. It's just that they have different skills. One looks better to us. But both look equally good to God *(because both did their best)*. But neither one should brag. Because neither is doing a perfect job.

Then what can we brag about? God says only one person can brag. That's Jesus. He can brag because he saved us and made us members of God's family.

Can You Believe It?

Do you know what this is? Maybe your parents have one of these for you, put away safely somewhere. This is a savings bond *(or whatever you have)*. Is it worth anything? If you didn't know what it was, you wouldn't think so. It isn't exactly the same thing as money. You couldn't take it down to the grocery store and spend it. A person who didn't know any better might even think it was just something worthless and throw it away.

What's really special about this document is that it has value because it's built on a promise. If this was one that your parents purchased for you when you were just born, it would mean that it is as many years old as you are. Your folks went to the bank *(or the insurance agent)* and gave some money in exchange for this document. Then the bank made a promise to keep the money safe, and to add some interest to it so that it would be even more valuable when you take it out again, and then someday when you're ready to take it out and use it, it will be waiting for you.

Object: *A U.S. Savings Bond certificate, or a bank savings deposit book, or an insurance policy.*

Now it all depends on keeping the promise. What if the banker *(or the insurance company)* decided not to keep the promise and just to keep the money? You would be the loser. And once in a while, but not very often, that actually happens. If we know and trust the banker we probably have nothing to worry about. But we have to remember to believe and trust the promise too.

Today the Bible story tells about a man like that. Abraham trusted God to keep a promise. God promised to give Abraham a child even though Abraham and his wife were very old. It seemed impossible, but Abraham believed God and trusted the promise. And it came true. Abraham knew he could trust God. His wife had her doubts, but Abraham believed. He didn't throw the promise away. We can trust God too. He will protect us in danger, give us strength to do what is right, and keep a special place for us with him in heaven. But we have to trust and believe that he will do it. And he will!

You Can
Flunk the Test

Today I want to tell you that I have something really valuable inside this envelope. I'm willing to share it with anybody who is interested. How many here would like to have a part of it? Fine. Now first, before I decide who gets some of what's inside, I want to give you a little test. You can just raise your hands when I ask the questions.

(Read from the clipboard:)

1. Raise your hand if you've always been kind and fair to your brothers and sisters and never done anything nasty to them.

2. Raise your hand if you've always tried to do what your parents want you to before they even get around to asking you to do it.

3. Raise your hand if you've always done everything you think God would want you to and have never forgotten to do the right thing.

Now, how many of you raised your hands all three times?

Objects: *A clipboard with an itemized list (see text below); A 9 x 12 manila envelope; A large certificate on heavy paper (for text, see below) which is inside the envelope.*

What I was really asking you was, have you always done everything perfectly right with no mistakes and never done anything wrong? Is there anybody here who can honestly say that you are like that? I know that there isn't anybody here like that because God tells us in the Bible that nobody is perfect except Jesus. All of us sin every day.

So does that mean I don't get to share the surprise with anybody here? Part of the surprise is that you don't have to pass the test to receive some of what's in the envelope. In fact, you can have part of it even if you flunk the test! And *everybody* flunks. *(Open the envelope, read:)*

"GUARANTEE: This promises that anybody who is not ashamed of Jesus is part of his family and will live with God forever in heaven. This promise applies especially to people who are full of mistakes."

That's what God promises us. He doesn't demand perfect people. He loves *us!*

It's Really Powerful!

I want you to imagine that in this little container I have something which, if I would inject it into your arm with this syringe, would make you very, very sick. Sometimes people who study medicine actually do this on purpose to see what they can learn about diseases and how to control them better. From the looks of this small bottle you can tell that if you could get really sick just from a little of what is in here, it's really powerful!

Now suppose after you caught the disease from this container I would take this second one here and some time later I would inject some of this into you. This would be the vaccine to cure you of the disease you received before. The same thing is true of the cure as is true of the disease. It doesn't take very much to do the job. Once again, it's really powerful. And lucky for us, the cure is more powerful than the disease. Over the centuries many people have died from

Objects: *Two small medicine bottles, clear glass, with a different color water in each bottle. The bottles are capped. If available you might also like to have a syringe to display (for injecting fluids into the body).*

---

diseases because no cure had yet been found. Today almost all diseases have cures. But we didn't have them soon enough to help people in the past. Or maybe a cure was available but a person didn't know about it. Or didn't want it. Or didn't believe it would help. People still die from diseases today. A lot of them wouldn't have to. That's why we try to get the good word out about the cures we have.

Sin is like disease. It only takes one person to start it. In the Bible Paul says just one person started trouble in the world (with some help and encouragement from the devil, of course). But the whole world has gotten sick. Without a cure we will die. But just one person brought the cure. That person is Jesus. By dying on the cross he has done enough to cure the entire world. His medicine is the strongest thing we know about. Let's make sure we keep in touch with Jesus, the doctor who cures us from sin.

Dead <u>and</u> Alive

Let's talk about flashlights. If you've ever been camping or hiking in the middle of the night you know how valuable a flashlight can be. They're safer than lanterns because you don't have to light them and they can't start fires. They're handy because they're fairly light and compact. You can pack them anywhere, or just stick them in your back pocket.

Now you'll notice this flashlight is very light *(pass it around)*. That's a bad sign, isn't it? That means there aren't any batteries in it. This flashlight doesn't have any life in it. It can't shine. Whoever manufactured this flashlight intended for us to use it to have light. If we never put any batteries in it we would have wasted our money buying the flashlight.

Now here are some batteries *(put in the dead ones)*. Funny thing, we still don't get any light. Why is that? Right. The batteries are dead. The flashlight is still worthless. Now let's try another set. *(Put in the live ones.)* Finally! Now the flash-

Object: *A flashlight with two sets of batteries, one set dead, the other alive.*

---

light can be what it is supposed to be. Now it can show you the path, signal for help, bring light in the darkness.

Flashlights do good things when they have life in them. God made us to be something like that. He created us to be helpers for the people around us, and to show how good and loving God is. But the devil wants to change us into God's enemies. The devil is very clever. He doesn't say "Stop being a servant." He even gets us to pretend we still are what we're supposed to be. He gets us to put dead batteries inside of ourselves. That happens when we forget about God. Then people think we will be what we really are not. God tells us to replace the dead batteries with live ones. God gave us live batteries when we were baptized. He made us his lights in the darkness. Now he says, "Don't swap the live batteries for dead ones. Get rid of what is dead and walk in newness of life!"

Let's Get an Expert

I'd like to invite all of you here to do something really exciting with me next Saturday morning. We're going up to the airport and I'll give everybody who comes along a free airplane ride. You see, I'm learning how to fly and I want you to enjoy the thrill of being up in the air. Now you may wonder how I can take you up in an airplane since I haven't had any flying lessons. Well, don't worry about that. I have a book here that I'm going to read, and then I'll take it along to the airport to refer to as we go along if I need it. It's called *(hold it up)* "The Do-It-Yourself Guide to Flying." I'll be able to save a lot of money with this book because I won't need to hire a flying instructor.

Now, let me see the hands. How many of you are ready to go with me? What's the matter, don't you like to fly? Don't you think it would be fun? What's that? You think we might crash?

You're probably right.

Nobody learns to fly by using a do-it-yourself method.

Object: *A book over which you have wrapped a tailored-to-fit dust cover (paper book jacket) on which you have written in large letters "The Do-it-Yourself Guide to Flying."*

Nobody can live successfully in this world and then go to heaven by using a do-it-yourself method either. If you or I would tell ourselves, "I don't need any help from God, I'm just going to go out and live a good life on my own," do you know what would happen? The same thing that happened to the Apostle Paul. In the Bible reading for today he tells us that he tried very hard to do what he thought were the right things. But he kept doing wrong things. Sometimes he didn't even know why he did what he did! He said "I do not understand my own actions." When he tried to love people he sometimes ended up hating them. The reason is that if we tell God we don't want any help, the devil will sneak in and mess everything up and pretty soon he has control of us. So we can't get along without an expert. We need God to give us guidance. Just like the person who learns how to fly an airplane had better get a flying instructor. Don't do it yourself!

All the Pain
Is Worth It

Have any of you had a new baby come to live in your family lately? You have probably seen how the baby grows and grows inside of mother until her stomach becomes very large. Sometimes we wonder how she can keep such a large package inside for nine long months. But that's the place where the baby can keep warm and be protected and get food to grow and become strong enough to be ready to live in the world. Sometimes mother gets very uncomfortable when she wants to walk and the baby is heavy. She can't run until it is born. It gets uncomfortable at night trying to sleep because you can't move around as much with a baby inside. And there are other things that happen inside mother to make her feel uncomfortable because the baby is growing.

(If an expectant mother is present, invite her to share some feelings.)

But we haven't even mentioned the most difficult part.

Objects: *This message may be given without any objects. The discussion will call to mind very real pictures for the children. You may, however, if possible have present a mother close to delivery time and/ or a newborn baby. If these are present, adjust the message in such a way that you involve and refer to them.*

After nine months, or sometimes a little longer, the baby is ready to come out. Usually this happens at the hospital, but if mother doesn't get there in time the baby can be born at home. Mother's body begins to work very hard to make the baby come out. This is called "labor" because it is very hard work. When the baby finally comes out it can be very painful. *(If a mother who has given birth is present, invite her to share.)*

But when it's all over, it's really wonderful. All the pain was worth it. The new bundle of life is like a miracle, so tiny and beautiful, and ready to grow up. It's a good thing mother is willing to put up with the pain.

Living in the world is like that for you and me too. There is pain and suffering all around us. We wonder why bad things have to happen to us. But God promises that one day pain and suffering will have gone and a new life will be ours.

I Can't
Do It Alone

I'll bet some of you have had these on your bicycle once when you were learning to ride a two-wheeler. I never had any when I first learned how. It was really painful trying to learn to balance. You push off from a wall or a step and at the beginning most of the time you end up crashing down on the grass (if you're lucky) or on the cement. Some children want to give up altogether and forget about learning to ride a two-wheel bike after all the failures they have. One little girl finally gave up trying and went inside. When her parents asked her how she was getting along she said, "Well, I'm really trying to learn how to ride it, but that old bike just doesn't trust me enough!"

That's why some parents put training wheels on their kids' bikes. Then the bike will stand up but the rider will get a feeling of how to begin to balance. Later on the training wheels can come off and the rider can balance without any trouble.

The training wheels are sort of an in-between solution.

Object: *A set of training wheels for use in helping children learn to ride a two-wheel bicycle.*

The wheels do the balancing for us. We end up saying "I can't do it alone." The wheels, if they could talk, would say "That's okay, I'll do it for you for a while. Then you can learn to do it yourself later on." It's almost as if the bike is doing the balancing because we don't know how.

That's something like what happens when we try to talk to God in our prayers. Have you ever felt like you just didn't know how to pray to God, you didn't know what he wanted to have you tell him, you didn't feel like you were getting through? Well guess what! Grown-ups feel that way too. The Apostle Paul, that great leader of the church, felt that way. He once said, "We do not know how to pray as we ought." But God gives us some "training wheels." The Holy Spirit helps us. The Spirit says, "I'll do it for you when you can't. I'll talk to the heavenly Father for you. I know what to say." The Holy Spirit is like our training wheels when we pray.

Why Did It Happen to Me?

How would you like to wear one of these as your main piece of clothing for a whole year? It could happen, you know. Sometimes kids no older than you are get so sick the doctor makes them stay in their house, or even in the hospital, for months and months at a time. Some of them never get dressed. They just keep their bathrobe handy. Some of them are not even that lucky. I know a girl who had an operation on her back. She had to stay in bed in a cast that held her rigid from her chin to her hips for months and months.

Why do things like that happen to people? If it happened to you or me we would probably say, "Why did it happen to me?" Why does God let it happen?

We don't know the answers. God doesn't tell us everything. Sometimes things happen that God wants to use to teach us something. Other times things happen that God doesn't like one bit. That's because the devil still has a lot of power and runs around causing trouble in the world. God

90

Object: *A bathrobe.*

---

doesn't like it any more than we do. But he lets it happen because he wants us to learn the difference between good and bad, and partly because it shows what terrible things can happen because sin is in the world.

But God doesn't just sit back and shake his head and say, "What a shame!" The Bible tells us a very special thing about God. He jumps right in, even into bad things that happen, and always makes some good thing come out of them too. Even when the devil seems to be winning, God uses it for some good thing. The Bible says, "We know that in everything God works for good with those who love him."

Think about that girl again, the one with the cast. She had to spend a lot of time in the hospital. But she met some people she would otherwise never have met. Some were still her good friends when she grew up. She had to have a wire put into her house from the public school. But she learned to listen carefully and to do things on her own. And her classmates learned something from it too. It wasn't all bad!

THE ELEVENTH SUNDAY AFTER PENTECOST

Safe, Safe, Safe

I'll bet you've seen a demonstration, maybe on television, showing how strong a certain kind of glue is. You remember when they demonstrate it they glue two pieces of wood together using the same kind of glue I have in this little container. And then they take a carpenter's clamp and tighten the pieces together, just like I'm doing now (of course the wood used in the demonstration is much larger).

And then comes the exciting part. In one example I remember two tractors were hooked up to the two chunks of wood, and they drove in opposite directions until they were pulling and straining for all they were worth. Do you remember what happens? The glue doesn't give up! In fact, the wood breaks apart, in other places and when they go back to pick up the pieces they find out that the place where the glue was is still tight and strong. Now that's real strength!

I guess you might say there's nothing that can separate that wood where the glue has put it together.

Objects: *A threaded clamp from a carpenter's or handy-man's workshop and a container of white glue. Also, two small plywood boards.*

That's the way it is with God. One of the most wonderful promises in the whole Bible is God's promise to us that there is nothing in the whole universe that can separate us from God's love. We are really safe in God's love. In fact, we're safe, safe, safe! The Apostle Paul found this to be true because he ran into so much danger but was never separated from God's love. God always keeps his promises. God's love is stronger than this glue, and that's pretty strong. Paul was so sure that we are safe in God's love that he lists the enemies that can't hurt us: death, things that bother us in the world right now, things that may come in the future that we don't even know about, anything in the whole creation. Isn't it wonderful to be able to live and not have to worry about losing God's love and protection? With God, we're safe, safe, safe!

They Hung Up

Have you ever had any fights with your relatives? I guess almost every family has sooner or later. It's pretty hard to keep on good terms with everybody. Sometimes it's even our fault there was a fight. If that's the case, we should get busy and straighten things out and ask others to forgive us.

But lots of times it's the problem of the others in the family —maybe an aunt or an uncle or some cousins, or even the grandparents. Maybe one of the reasons we have so much difficulty keeping on good terms with our relatives is because we are so close to each other and we know each other so well. Lots of times we are unkind to the people we are closer to. You notice it happening with your brothers and sisters, don't you? Often we treat them much worse than we would a neighbor or a visitor in our house. Sometimes we are mean to our brothers and sisters right in front of the visitors!

Well I want you to imagine that I have had a disagreement with my brother who lives across town from me. Not long

Object: *A telephone, either a plastic one (princess phone size) or a real one that will unplug, allowing you to carry it with you.*

---

ago we argued about something and we just couldn't agree. He got mad and told me to take my family and go home (we were in his living room at the time). I was really surprised but I finally did it. Now we are planning a family picnic for all the brothers and sisters and cousins. I'm calling him to invite him. Let's see what happens:

(Dial a number and let it ring on the other end): "Hello, Mark, this is your *(brother/sister, give your name)*. Listen, I'm sorry about last week.... Now before you say anything I want to tell you something important.... We're having a picnic in the city park on Saturday ... a family reunion. We want all of your family to be sure and come. Will you? ... Mark? ... Hello? ..."

Guess what! He hung up! You see how hard it is to put things back together sometimes? The Apostle Paul had trouble achieving harmony in the early church. Even though it was difficult—at times impossible—he never stopped trying.

It's Still Good

Take a look at this dollar bill. It's really had rough treatment, hasn't it? Sometimes when you go through the line at the supermarket and they make change you end up with a dollar bill like this. There's no telling who did the damage or why, but the damage has been done.

Suppose you went to the bank and wanted to put this dollar bill into your savings account. But the teller at the window takes a look at it and gives it back and says, "Oh, I'm sorry, you'll just have to keep that now. You see, it's been wrinkled so badly that it doesn't have any value any more. Sorry!"

Do you think the banker would do that? No, he wouldn't. You see, the dollar bill is really a promise that the government makes to give us the value that the money represents. It is worth so much silver. And the government, and the bankers, have a rule that if you bring in a dollar bill that

Object: *A dollar bill that has been damaged (torn). Your local banker can probably loan you one that has been torn in two pieces (in exchange for a good one).*

---

isn't really fit to be used any more, they will simply replace it with another one. Then they will take your damaged bill and destroy it so nobody else has to deal with it. So the value isn't cancelled just because somebody misuses the dollar bill.

God makes promises too. His are even better than the government's, or the bank's, because his guarantee is better and lasts forever, even after all the governments and banks are gone. When God makes a promise that he will love somebody, he doesn't change his mind if we laugh at the promise or forget about it or try to throw it away. When we were baptized God promised to keep us in his family. We could take our baptismal certificate and punch holes in it or burn it up, but the promise is still good. When God promises to love us he keeps his promise forever.

What a
Mighty Mind!

I want to have you hold out your hands in front of you. Now look at the back sides of them while you make your fingers move. Move them slowly, in and out, up and down. Watch how the little connecting rods in your hand work when you do it. Isn't your hand a marvelous little machine!

Now start moving your hand all around, in every direction you can. Watch how it can move on the end of your arm. Can you imagine how many different bones and muscles and other kinds of connectors are necessary to make that wrist move in all those directions? Imagine you had to make a machine in a laboratory that could move in all those directions, as smoothly and efficiently, as your own wrist. It's really amazing, isn't it!

Now take your two hands and place them up at the back of your head, feeling the shape of it. Underneath this part of you is your brain. You can get an idea about how big it is and what shape it is. Your brain is a fantastic computer center. The scientists tell us that the human brain is a more complicated computer center than anything that has ever been invented.

In your brain there are hundreds of little grooves, like the grooves on a phonograph record. Just like the phonograph record, your brain records information in the grooves, and when you are ready to remember it there it is all stored and ready. Isn't that amazing! And the information recorded in your brain is not exactly the same as that in any other brain in the world.

What a mighty mind it must have taken to do these wonderful kinds of things. And when you look at the creation all around us you see more and more of the same kinds of unbelievable miracles. The mighty mind that did it, of course, is God. When we realize how amazing his mind must be we don't have to worry about wanting answers from him for all the things we don't understand. We don't even appreciate the things he does that we *do* understand. We should be content just to be thankful for the answers God gives and not demand more than he tells us. Oh how deep are God's riches and wisdom and knowledge! What a mighty mind he must have!

God Has a Better Idea

Kids, have you ever made something with clay and a mold? I have one here today. Now suppose you had an art teacher at school who gave you an assignment to do at home over the weekend. And the assignment is to make a *(name whatever design you have)* out of clay and bring it to class on Monday. And so you go home and remember as you are coming in the door that you already have this cookie cutter with exactly the same design as the teacher asked for. So you just decide to do a quick, easy job of making one like this *(shape the clay into the cookie cutter)* and you'll save time having to think up a way to design it besides! And it comes out like this *(show them the finished product)*.

Now, how would you feel about taking a piece of art like this to school? How do you think the teacher would feel? If you're like me, and if you know teachers like the ones I

Objects: *Some playdough or modeling clay, about half of which is in a rough lump. Also, a cookie cutter which makes a design such as a star, a deer, a tree, or something similar. The other half of the dough or clay should be shaped, in advance, into a creative but free-flowing version of the design represented by the cookie cutter.*

---

know, you'd say, "This isn't satisfactory." Sure, it technically is the correct design. But it doesn't represent me. It represents somebody else. And the design somebody else gave me wasn't all that fancy and creative and artistic, besides!

No, we would do a lot better by saying, "I have a better idea." And you could do something like this *(show them your artwork)*. Now the one I did by myself may not be perfect, but it's worth more because I didn't just use somebody else's mold.

God doesn't want us to use other people's molds either when we live our lives. We should listen to God's instructions instead, because God has a better idea. One of the molds people try to use on us is saying, "Everybody is doing it; you have to do it too." But God has a better idea. He says, "Do what is good. Don't get molded. Be different!"

Who's In Charge Here?

Do you ever get tired of other people telling you what to do? Your parents always have directions, don't they? And there are other adults or older people who have a right, or think they have a right, to tell us what we should do. Everywhere you look there are rules to follow, laws to obey, directions to follow, and penalties to pay if you don't do what you're told.

Suppose you could be your own lawmaker. Suppose you could be the police or the sheriff. Suppose you had the right to wear one of these *(put on the hat or the badge)*. Wouldn't that be great? Then you could do what you wanted to, couldn't you? You could decide which rules to obey and which to ignore. Maybe you could even change some rules. You could make it rough for people who aren't nice to you.

Of course, if we're going to be fair about this, if we allow you to be your own lawmaker, we should allow your friends to be their own lawmakers too, shouldn't we? Now what

Object: *A policeman's hat or a sheriff's badge (if you can't borrow either, construct a reasonable facsimile of a badge and cover it with foil).*

---

would *that* be like? You make your rules, your neighbors make their rules, somebody else makes other rules. Pretty soon we'd have confusion wouldn't we? Nobody would agree. You couldn't tell somebody else how to behave because they would be using their own set of rules. And they couldn't make their rules work because you wouldn't listen. And not only that, every one of you might use your power to punish people who shouldn't be punished. You might just get even with people because you didn't like what they did, or make it hard for them because you didn't like their looks.

Somebody has to be in charge. And you know, even a policeman or a sheriff isn't really "in charge." He only enforces laws handed down from somebody else. The government makes the laws, and the Supreme Court controls them. And all of these groups do the best they can. But the only laws that are perfect, completely fair and good are the laws of God.

It's Not
Ours to Keep

Every once in a while we read some amazing stories in the newspapers about people who locked themselves up in their house and never came out to live with the rest of the world. In one story not long ago a very old man died in his house, where he lived all alone. When the doctor checked him he found the man had simply starved himself to death. But under his bed there were thousands of dollars in cash that could have fed him comfortably for years and years. The old man had just decided to live to himself and pretend the rest of the world wasn't there.

A lot of people do that sort of thing, even though they come out of their house during the daytime. Here is a strongbox such as some people have in their homes. I have a key here and when I open it up you can see that inside there are some valuable papers that need to be protected. This strongbox and what it has inside are something like the old man who starved to death. We can use our hiding places to

Objects: *A strongbox, with a key, in which are some valuable papers (perhaps a will, life insurance policies, bonds).*

---

put our valuable things so that nobody else can get them. Now there's nothing wrong with saving some valuable things if they are put away safely to help others. But when we do it simply because we want to protect ourselves from the rest of the world we will end up just like the sad old man. After we die somebody else will find our valuables and will have to decide what to do with them.

And the strangest part is that no matter how well we hide away our valuables, or even ourselves (when we don't share our lives with others) our possessions are not ours to keep. They are all given to us on loan from God. We are not to collect things and keep them for ourselves only. We aren't in this world to live only to ourselves. We're here to use what God loaned us to share with others. That includes our lives, our abilities, and all the good things we can do to make the world better for everybody. Whether we live or whether we die we are the Lord's. Let's live that way.

What's in the Cards?

Did you know there are people who think they can tell the future of a person by using cards? When you hear someone say, "It won't happen because it just isn't in the cards!" this is what they mean. Well, I don't really believe you can tell the future with cards, but let's just do a little pretending. I have here in my hand a very special set of cards. On each one there is a description that could describe your future. I want everyone here to pick a card and let's see how you would feel about what you end up with. *(Have everybody pick, then have them each tell what theirs says and how they would feel about it. Repeat their answers so the congregation can get the message too.)*

Now I should tell you that some of the cards described things that most people would think were pretty good and some of the cards described things that sound pretty bad. So it was just good or bad luck if you received one kind or

Object: *A deck of cards you have prepared from stiff paper or file cards. On each write one thing that could be someone's future: examples could be Married, Bank President, Garbage Collector, No Friends, Famous Actor, Hardly Any Money.*

---

the other. But a little of that goes on in real life too, doesn't it? How many people do you know who have a lot of advantages because they were in the right place at the right time? And how many people do you know who struggle along in life because they just "didn't get the breaks"? Some of that is really true.

But now, the important thing for us as Christians, is how and what we do with what life hands out to us? Do you realize that there is not a single thing on these cards that God could not use for good? Even if you end up with no money at all you could have a really good life for God. That's what St. Francis did. He was one of the finest examples of Christian living we have. In the Bible the Apostle Paul says, "For me to live is Christ, to die is gain." He knew that whatever God hands us, he can do something good with it.

Just Like Us

How many of you have heard the story of the *Prince and the Pauper?* This is a famous story written by Mark Twain. Sometimes you can see versions of it on television. If you know the story you know that the young prince who was in line to become the next King of England met a young beggar boy one day who looked exactly like himself. The beggar always wanted to know how it would feel to live in a nice house and the prince wanted to know how ordinary people really live. So they changed clothes and swapped places for a while. Instead of this *(hold up the crown)* the prince decided to dress up in clothes that looked as ragged as these do *(display the clothing)*.

We don't need to retell the whole story here but the important thing for us to notice this time is that the prince couldn't get back to the palace when he wanted to because the guards really thought the other boy was the prince and they thought the real prince was a beggar. So instead of having an inter-

Objects: *A crown, made from cardboard and covered with gold or aluminum foil (check your 3-kings props from the Christmas supply closet) and some old, dirty, workworn clothes.*

---

esting day in the city, the prince actually had to live among the poor for a while, and find out what starvation was like, and get beat up by the beggar's real father, and learn to steal for a living. When it was all over and he finally got back (you have to read the story to learn the surprise ending of how he did that) he really did appreciate how poor people feel. And he could be a better prince and king afterwards.

That's what Jesus did. He didn't just peek into the world and say, "Oh, my goodness, it looks like they have a few problems down there." IIe actually took off the crown *(pick it up again)* and traded it for a while for dirty clothes. He became a servant and suffered like we do every day. That way he showed us that he knows what we have to go through, and he helped us to know that his love for us isn't just an easy thing to say but a hard, painful thing to deliver to us. He came and lived in the world just like us. So now we have a special friend in heaven.

Ready for Anything

As you can see, I'm ready to go camping. I have my pack all put together and I'm ready for anything. Maybe you'd like to see what I have. *(Open the pack and start taking out the items. Comment on why you think each will be helpful, and if you wish, involve the group by passing each around so the group can handle and examine them.)*

Now can anybody think of anything I've forgotten? You know, it seems as if no matter how well you pack there is always something you can forget. I remember hearing about a camper who got all the way out into the wilds with a pack so complete you couldn't imagine he'd ever be needing anything. And then he discovered he'd forgotten to bring along his matches!

It's a lucky thing you and I don't have to carry a full pack like this around with us day by day. That would get mighty tiresome. But we can still be ready for anything even if we don't carry one of these. That's because God has already

Object: *A backpack such as boy scouts or hikers use. Fill it with all kinds of necessary equipment—flashlight, first aid kit, hatchet, dehydrated trail food (optional), rope, etc. You might even add a few seemingly ridiculous "ready-for-anything" items.*

---

given us the one piece of equipment we need. It's his faithful love and protection. God promised a long time ago that he would never give up on us and that he would help us to make it through the tough places of this world. Just like the rough thickets a hiker has to get through, or the steep trails or cliffs, or the dangerous water crossings, our life is full of times and places that really scare us sometimes. But God promises to be faithful. His love and protection are always here. That's worth celebrating and shouting "hooray!" about. That's why the Apostle Paul tells us that no matter what kind of rough going we get into we can forget what lies behind and strain forward to what lies ahead. Paul was ready for anything and we can be too. We don't have to be anxious. We can be at peace in our heart and our mind. God has given us a spiritual backpack that's so perfect and complete that we're ready for anything. Let's remember to tell God "Thanks!" for doing it.

Someone's Here to Help

I really like eating nuts. Almonds are really tasty and the shells aren't too hard to open. Walnuts are good too, but the shells are a little tougher. But Brazil nuts are the hardest nuts I know to crack open. I need a volunteer this time to help me. *(Try to encourage someone who will have a hard time cracking a brazil nut without help.)* Will you crack this nut for us please? We'll put the shells here in the dish. *(If this person succeeds, say thank you and ask others until you find one who can't do it.)*

Now what do we do when we can't get the shell off? One thing you could do would be to just give up. Or you could hope that somebody else would come along and crack the nuts. But in the first case you wouldn't get to eat the nuts, and in the second case you might not either—because usually people who crack nuts like to eat them themselves.

Let's try something *(ask the volunteer who couldn't crack*

Objects: *A nutcracker, some brazil nuts, and a plate or dish to catch the shells.*

---

the nut): will you come back over here a minute? Now put your hands on the nutcracker, with the nut inside, the way you usually do. Now try it, and I'm going to put my hands right on top of yours and together we will crack it open. There, you see it works when someone's here to help.

Guess what. Someone's here to help us do all the difficult things that we have to do. If you have a hard job to do, or if somebody asked you for assistance but it sounds like a lot of work to you, or if you need to apologize to somebody when it feels hard to do, or help somebody you don't like very well, there is always somebody here to help. The biggest mistake we make when we try to be faithful to Jesus is trying to do what he wants all by ourselves. Jesus says, "Ask me to help. I'm available. Let's do it together." Jesus gives us strength and power to get the work done. The Bible says, "I can do all things through Christ who strengthens me."

For Love
or Money

I want to tell you about two boys. They were walking down the sidewalk in the middle of a busy city one day when one of them noticed that a small child was wandering down over the curb and out toward the busy traffic. The boy yelled to his partner, "Look, he could get killed! Let's go!" and together they raced to the rescue, snatching the child and bringing him safely to the curb.

The mother, who had accidentally gotten separated from her child on the busy sidewalk, now came rushing up and after giving her child a hug to see that he was safe, turned to the two boys. "Oh, how can I ever repay you!" she begged them. Then she offered them a money reward. The first boy accepted the reward, feeling he had earned it. The second boy said, "Oh, no, I don't want a reward. I was glad to do it. Please keep the money."

Both of these boys did exactly the same kind of rescue. Both of them did a good and valuable deed. But they did the deed for different reasons. Both wanted to help the child

Objects: *An empty billfold and an offering plate*

(that's what made the action good). But one wanted a reward. The other didn't need one.

Those are the two main reasons most of us have for doing good things. Some of us do them for love, some of us do them for money. Some people think that God wants us to do good things to prove we are good enough to be in his family. If we do them he will reward us, like putting money into this empty billfold. But Christians know that God already gave us the best reward of all—his love. So now we can do good things without looking for a reward. We can tell people who want to pay us for our help, "Just put it in the offering plate. We already have our reward. Jesus loves and died for us." The Apostle Paul praised the people he wrote to because he said when they did good things they did them as a "labor of love." They weren't trying to get a reward. They already knew God loved them. That was enough. Now they could do good just because God's love flowed through them. We can do the same thing!

It Goes
a Long Way

I want to tell one of you a secret *(whisper into an ear "Jesus loves you").* Now, did anybody here get that message besides the person I whispered to? Well, let's pass the message along. Now I want this person, who just received the message, to whisper to someone else, and that person say it in a whisper to someone else, until everyone gets the message. *(Take a half minute for this.)*

Now I think you'll all agree that this is a special, personal kind of message that doesn't need to be shouted. It needs to be delivered with care, from one ear to another. But now there's one problem. There are a lot of people here today who still don't know the message. So I'm going to whisper it to them too. *(Whisper "Jesus loves us" loudly enough into the microphone so that the congregation can hear it.)* Now, will you folks in the back raise your hand if you heard the message? *(If they didn't hear it, whisper it louder, but not in spoken voice.)*

Object: *A microphone, hooked up to the sound system with amplifier on. (If this equipment is not available, a megaphone could be used.)*

Why all this whispering? Well, I want you to think about spreading God's good news to other people. The best way is not to shout it to people. The best way is to set a good example. So you see you could get the message to others by doing what Jesus wants us to do for them. But at the same time we need to say something about Jesus. Jesus is the one who makes us want to do good things. And the amazing thing is that if we spread the good news of Jesus by living faithful lives for him, the message will get out far beyond us. It goes a long way, just like the message went over the microphone today and spread all over the church. Now the microphone and the wires and the speakers are something like what God does through his Holy Spirit. What the Spirit does through us gets carried all over the city and the country.

That's what happened to Paul's friends at Thessalonica. Paul said to them, "Your faith in God has gone forth everywhere!" Ours can do the same.

117

We'll Meet Again

We live in a world where a lot of people move from one house to another, from one town to another, from one state to another. How many of you here have moved at least once that you can remember?

You know how it feels when a neighbor family moves away and your best friend, the one you always liked to play with the best, goes away to live in another city. We are upset and depressed about it for a long time. It's like grieving for somebody. We know they are gone and we are going to miss them terribly. But it's something we have to get used to because it happens from time to time.

Now let's suppose that you have a neighbor who is your best friend and one day your friend tells you that they are moving *(open the map)*. Their family is going from *(point to your town)* to *(trace your finger to another city at the other end of your state; if you live in a small state, pick a city in a neighboring state)*. It really doesn't matter, you know, if they move one city away or the whole country away, because if

Object: *A map of the United States.*

---

you don't get to see your friend anymore it's like losing someone forever.

Now let's suppose about six months after your friend moves away that your dad comes home from work and announces to you that your family is moving from *(point out your town)* to *(trace a line to a city as far away in continental United States as you can find).* Now you have more problems, because this time it isn't one friend that is leaving you but it's you that's leaving all the rest of your friends. That can be pretty painful. But when you get unloaded in your new home in the new city over here, what do you find? Lo and behold, your old friend, who moved away six months ago, is now living only two blocks away in your new city! Hard to believe? Sometimes it happens!

That's the way it is with God and us. Sometimes we lose friends who die. But even they are not gone forever. They go to live with God. And when we die someday, we will live with God as well. It's not good-bye forever. God says we'll meet again!

119

It Could
Be Tomorrow

Boys and girls, what have I here? This is a calendar, but not the kind that some of you are used to seeing. This one doesn't hang on the wall. It sits on the top of the desk. It's useful because while you're doing your work if you suddenly think of something you can jot it down right on the page with the correct date. So, for instance, if I wanted to remember somebody's birthday in this group *(ask several to tell you their birthdays)*, I'll just find your date and write in the information in red ink, for a red-letter day! Now, someone else? Let's write down your birthday too. And someone else? *(Write down as many birthdays as you like.)*

Now, I'm going to turn back to today's date and show you *(hold it so all can see the pages)* how I can be reminded of coming events. I simply turn the pages like this and pretty soon we know we will come to one of your birthdays. If I keep looking ahead like this it will remind me when to get a birthday card for one of you, won't it. And there might be

Object: *A calendar, the type which shows one small page for each day, with the pages on a holder, with metal rods through the punch-holes of each page. On one of the pages, about 10 days ahead of today's date, write or clip a note which says "Jesus is coming back today!" in red ink. Then open the calendar to today's date. Keep your red pen handy.*

---

other important things written in here to remember too, such as . . . oh my goodness, what is this? It says "Jesus is coming back today!" Why, that's only ten days from now! Did you know that? Did you know Jesus is coming back in ten days? That's what it says right here!

Do you believe it? Do you think Jesus is coming back in ten days? How do you suppose that got into my calendar? Even if it's wrong, if it's a mistake, do you think it's possible? Could Jesus come back in ten days and end the world if he wanted to? Right! He could! In fact, it could be tomorrow!

Now let's ask, what would you do if you knew Jesus would be coming in ten days? *(Field some answers.)* The Bible tells us to be ready for Jesus to return at any time. Any page on this calendar could be the right one. We should always be watchful, doing as much of God's work as we can now in case the time runs out before we're ready.

I'll Give
You Myself

In many churches there is a practice that families take turns giving the flowers for the altar on Sunday. Then when the last worship service is over the family which gave the flowers can take them home and enjoy them at their house. Sometimes the flowers are given on special times of the year because that's the time someone in the family is having a birthday or a wedding anniversary. So the pastor puts a few words in the bulletin mentioning the flowers and the special event, and then the flowers go home for that person to enjoy.

Now let's suppose that I gave the flowers you see here on the altar today. And I gave them because today is my wedding anniversary. After church I plan to take them home and we will enjoy them at our house as a reminder of the special event. But as I am coming up to the altar after shaking the pastor's hands I see you still sitting in your pew with your head down. I step closer and notice that you are crying silently to yourself. So I sit down and we talk a little while and you tell me that your best friend is in the hospital.

Object: *One of the vases of altar flowers (they can be referred to without moving them out of place)*

Now I decide that maybe I don't need these flowers so badly after all. So I invite you to take the flowers along to the hospital and share them with your friend. He might appreciate them much more than I would right now. You are happy that I was willing to share them so you stop crying and dry your tears, put a smile on your face, but still stay sitting in the pew.

So now I ask you, "Is there anything else I can do?" And then you tell me that it is difficult to visit your friend because he is very ill and may never recover. You tell me that you are really afraid to go and visit because you don't know what to say. And so I promise I will go with you to visit him. And that really makes you feel happy.

Sometimes we need to give our friends more than flowers or gifts. Sometimes we need to give ourselves. That's what Paul did, too, for the people in Thessalonica.

Greater and Greater

Have you ever stopped to think what wonderful things sponges are? They seem rather ordinary to most of us. We have them around the house, although most of them are tucked away under the sink or in the garage until we're ready to scrub the floor or wash the car or maybe do the dishes. But a sponge can do some things no scrub cloth can do.

Here is a sponge from my kitchen (*let a few examine it*). It's very dry and hard and light. In its present shape it isn't very useful. But now if I take this sponge and put it into this bowl and pour this water on it, look what I have! The sponge changes and grows greater and greater until it has "drunk up" all of this water. Now the sponge is ready for action. I can lift it up, and notice how if I'm careful hardly any of the water is spilled, and it can scrub the car or the floor or the dishes and the water is delivered from the sponge to the place where it is most needed. And when we press harder, more water comes out.

Objects: *A large sponge, a large bowl, and a pitcher of water.*

Isn't the sponge a marvelous thing!

Sometimes we talk about people as being "sponges" and we don't mean it in a nice way. We mean they're selfish and they soak up what they want from everybody else and never give anything in return. But it doesn't have to be that way. You can be a giving sponge too. In fact, in the Bible Paul tells us all to be something like a sponge. He tells us to soak up all the love God gives us, like a sponge soaks up water. But then comes the next step. He tells us to overflow with that love. He wants us to go to work and share what we have received by overflowing with love and pouring it out for others. Don't worry if you get empty doing this. God will fill you up again. His pitcher never gets empty. Let's ask God to help us share his love both with one another and with all people! Be a giving sponge.

Free at Last

Everybody who has ever been arrested, raise your hand so we can see how many of us have. What? Nobody? Nobody here has ever gone to jail? Well, I can't tell you about the Bible story today until I can find someone who has been arrested. So, I'll tell you what I'll do. I need a volunteer. *(Choose somebody you know will be a good sport whether they volunteer or not.)* Now, you just stand right here for a minute, and hold your hands behind your back *(snap on the handcuffs or tie his or her hands securely).*

Oh, I forgot to ask you. What was it that you did that made you deserve to be arrested? You don't know? You don't think you should be arrested? Don't you think I could think of something you should be arrested for? If I could find your parents out there in the church I'll bet they could tell me something—do you think so?

Now, I'm going to give the key to your handcuffs to this person *(pick someone and give it to them).* Only that person has the power to unlock your wrists *(or untie the rope).* But let's pretend that person wants to keep you trapped as long

Objects: *A pair of handcuffs and a key (if you cannot secure these you could use a piece of sturdy cord).*

---

as possible. What could you do then? You'd have to find a friend who was stronger than the one who has power over you, wouldn't you!

When Jesus came into this world he told us that the devil had put handcuffs on us but that he would take the key away from Satan. When Jesus died on the cross it looked like Jesus had changed his mind. Some people thought Satan had put handcuffs on Jesus that day! But when Jesus arose from the dead, guess what? He came back with the key! He unlocked our handcuffs and set us free to live for him.

You know, there are still people today who don't know that Jesus has the key to their life. They keep living as though the devil were in charge. When Jesus comes back at the end of the world there will be no doubt in anybody's mind: Jesus has the key to everybody's life. That's what we celebrate today, on this Sunday called "Christ the King." *(Free the child's hands.)* But we don't have to wait that long to be free in Christ. Jesus has already set us free to be in his family. Isn't that great news?